# The Purpose of Theosophy

Also in this series:

Theosophy and the Search for Happiness
*Texts by Moon Laramie and Annie Besant*

Art and Theosophy
*Texts by Martin Firrell and A.L. Pogosky*

Theosophy and Esoteric Christianity
*Texts by Isis Resende, R. Heber Newton
& Franz Hartmann*

Theosophy and Yoga
*Texts by Jenny Baker and Annie Besant*

Theosophy and Social Justice
*Texts by Dr. Barbara B. Hebert, William Quan Judge
& Annie Besant*

Forthcoming:

Theosophy and Clairvoyance
*Texts by Kurt Leland and C.W. Leadbeater*

# The Purpose of Theosophy

Texts by
Petra Meyer &
Patience Sinnett

**martin firrell company**
MODERN THEOSOPHY

First published in 2019 by Martin Firrell Company Ltd
10 Queen Street Place, London EC4R 1AG, United Kingdom.

ISBN 978-1-912622-22-1

Design © Copyright Martin Firrell Company 2020.
Introduction © Copyright Moon Laramie 2020.
Essay © Copyright Petra Meyer 2020.

All rights reserved. No part of this publication may be reproduced, stored in or introduced into a retrieval system, or transmitted, in any form, or by any means (electronic, mechanical, photocopying, recording or otherwise) without the prior written consent of the publisher.

This book is sold subject to the condition that it shall not, by way of trade or otherwise, be lent, re-sold, hired out, or otherwise circulated without the publisher's prior consent in any form of binding or cover other than that in which it is published and without a similar condition including this condition being imposed on the subsequent purchaser.

Text is set in Baskerville, 12pt on 18pt.

Baskerville is a serif typeface designed in 1754 by John Baskerville (1706–1775) in Birmingham, England. Compared to earlier typeface designs, Baskerville increased the contrast between thick and thin strokes. Serifs were made sharper and more tapered, and the axis of rounded letters was placed in a more vertical position. The curved strokes were made more circular in shape, and the characters became more regular.

Baskerville is categorised as a transitional typeface between classical typefaces and high contrast modern faces. Of his own typeface, John Baskerville wrote, 'Having been an early admirer of the beauty of letters, I became insensibly desirous of contributing to the perfection of them. I formed to myself ideas of greater accuracy than had yet appeared, and had endeavoured to produce a set of types according to what I conceived to be their true proportion.'

# Introduction
by Moon Laramie

The Theosophical Society was formed in New York on 17 November 1875 by H. P. Blavatsky, Henry Steel Olcott and William Quan Judge. The society has three fundamental objects at its core:

*To form a nucleus of universal brotherhood without distinction of race, creed, sex, caste or colour.*

*To encourage the study of comparative religion, philosophy and science.*

*To investigate the unexplained laws of nature and the powers latent in man.*

Petra Meyer explains that the original purposes of the society were 'to revive the wisdom tradition of the ancients, to counteract widespread materialism, and help each human being to discover his or her true and eternal Higher Self again'. In *The Key To Theosophy*, Madame Blavatsky states that theosophy 'is as old as the world in its teachings and… is also the broadest and most catholic system of all.' She goes on to add that theosophy is not a religion, but 'is Divine Knowledge or Science'.

In her article on the purpose of theosophy, Patience Sinnett writes, 'In the formation of the Theosophical Society the founders were acting under the direct wishes of certain of the Mahatmas, who thus opened the occult door a little way for those whose intuitions were sufficiently active to guide them to take advantage of this source of knowledge.' C. Jinarajadasa refers to these same Mahatmas or Masters of the Wisdom when he describes theosophy as 'a revelation of a knowledge to those who have not yet discovered it by those who have already done so.' He insists that theosophy requires no strict adherence to any rigid doctrine: 'Though in its fundamental ideas Theosophy is a revelation, there is no authority in it to an individual, unless he himself assents to it.'[1]

Theosophy takes the view that there exists a 'prisca theologia', a universal truth that is threaded through all the world's religions. Patience Sinnett remarks that the simple lives and moral codes of Buddha, Jesus and other great teachers 'varied so little that it is hardly difficult for students to see that their knowledge must have been drawn from the same source, although they lived at very different periods of time'.

This is echoed in Geoffrey Farthing's comment that 'all real truths synthesize into One Truth.'[2] Petra Meyer points out that this 'One Truth' has for generations remained deliberately hidden from 'a world too selfish and too much attached to the objects of the senses'.

Patience Sinnett argues that theosophy enables the individual 'to grasp intellectually the fact that every thing connected with corporeal life on this planet is but transitory, therefore, not the real'. This is an area where theosophy and modern science have begun to converge. As Petra Meyer observes, 'Since the discovery of the illusionary nature of matter… many of today's scientists express a very mystical world view… In modern physics, these are the realms of the atomic and sub-atomic world, in mysticism they are non-ordinary states of consciousness, in which the everyday sensory world is transcended.'

Herein lies the importance of theosophy in the 21st Century. Its modern relevance is perhaps best summed up by author and former head of the Theosophical Society in Pasadena, Gottfried de Purucker: 'The Esoteric Tradition, today called theosophy, may be proved to be this formulation of the truth. It deals with the universe, and with man as an offspring of that universe… It teaches us how to understand men, and enables us to go behind the veil of outer appearances into the realms of reality.'[3]

1. C. Jinarajadasa, *Practical Theosophy*, Theosophical Publishing House, 1918.

2. Geoffrey Farthing, *Theosophy What's It All About?* Theosophical Publishing House, 1967.

3. Gottfried de Purucker, *The Esoteric Tradition*, Theosophical University Press, 1935.

Petra Meyer

Petra Meyer is the President of the Blavatsky Lodge in England. She was born in 1947 in Essen, Germany where she also grew up. After leaving school, she started an apprenticeship with a chemical company in her home town and, after graduating, worked in their legal department for several years. The company was based next to an abattoir and this prompted her to question the existence of a god who wanted animals to be slaughtered in this way for food.

She became a vegetarian. She did intensive research into early Christianity, discovered that Jesus came from the Brotherhood of the Essenes, and that their teachings differed profoundly in many ways from the traditional Bible.

The first time she became aware of the Theosophical Society was in a vegetarian magazine where she found an advertisement for a book trilogy called *Das Theosophische Weltbild* (*A Theosophical Picture of the World*). The author was the German theosophist, Beatrice Flemming. Petra contacted Flemming because she had several questions, and from then on a firm friendship developed between them. Flemming was already in her 80s and Petra was half her age. Flemming had lectured widely on theosophical subjects and Petra benefitted greatly from her wisdom.

In 1984, Petra moved with her husband and two children to London where she still lives. Beatrice Flemming had given her the address of the Theosophical Bookshop which was at that time in a side street opposite the British Museum. They gave her the address of the Theosophical Society in Gloucester Place and she joined in May 1991. In 1992, she became a member of the Blavatsky Lodge.

When Beatrice Flemming died in 1986, she left Petra her personal accounts of her life as a theosophist including her experiences of the Holocaust during World War II.

In 1997, Petra Meyer's husband suffered two brain haemorrhages which left him completely disabled. She looked after him until his death in 2010. In 2011, she began once more to participate and contribute to the work of the Blavatsky Lodge. She became Programme Secretary in 2016 and President in 2017. She has lectured on a range of topics including the Book of Dzyan, the vegetarian origins of Christianity, the wisdom of Lao Tzu and the discipline of Tai Chi, and Jesus and the Brotherhood of the Essenes. She has lectured at the Theosophical Society in England's Summer School and also at the European School of Theosophy on subjects ranging from reincarnation to eastern mysticism and modern science.

# The Purpose of Theosophy
by Petra Meyer (2019)

*Theosophy is who Theosophy does, not thinks, not studies, not feels but does.* Helena Petrovna Blavatsky.

In 1889, in New York, Madame Blavatsky published a small book called *The Voice of the Silence*. This book contains fragments from a very old composition of texts with the title *The Book of the Golden Precepts*, a collection of treatises originating from Buddhist and pre-Buddhist sources. It is one of the works which were only given to students of mysticism in the East and therefore remained unknown by scholars and the general public.

*The Voice of the Silence* is a translation of three treatises taken from these old writings. In the preface, it is pointed out that the six schools of philosophy in India differ according to their Masters. Beyond the Himalayas, the methods in esoteric schools do not differ, unless the 'Guru' is simply a Lama, little more learned than those he teaches.

The *Book of Dzyan*, on which Madame Blavatsky's *The Secret Doctrine* is based, also belongs to the same series. She tells us that the original precepts are engraved on thin oblong squares, but that copies are very often on discs, and that these discs are generally preserved on the altars of temples attached to the Mahayana (Yogachara) schools.[1] They are variously written, sometimes in Tibetan, but mostly in ideographs taken from Senzar, a name for the secret sacerdotal language or the 'Mystery-speech' of the initiated adepts all over the world. Madame Blavatsky says that all of the precepts could not be given out to a world too selfish and too much attached to the objects of the senses because, unless man is serious in the pursuit of self-knowledge, he will never listen. Therefore only a few judicious selections were chosen which were best suited for the few true mystics in the Theosophical Society to help answer their needs.

Although, like the Upanishads and the Bhagavad Gita, extracts of the ethics of *The Book of the Golden Precepts* fill volumes in Eastern literature, only a real mystic will appreciate the words of Krishna-Christos, or the Higher Self. In the Bhagavad Gita, for example, we can read: 'Sages do not grieve for the Living nor the Dead. Never did I not exist, nor you, nor these rulers of men; nor will any one of us ever hereafter cease to be. 'This wisdom is also echoed in the 'Hymn of Creation' which appears in the Rigveda (The word 'Rigveda' means, literally, 'praise and knowledge'). The four Vedas are a collection of ancient Indian Sanskrit hymns of which the Rigveda is the first and most important. It deals with the creation of the Universe and was given to the world thousands of years ago by great sages at Lake Man(a)sarovar, a high altitude freshwater lake fed by the Kailash Glaciers near Mount Kailash in Tibet. In *The Secret Doctrine*, H.P. Blavatsky quotes the following lines, crediting them to the Rigveda:

> *Who knows the secret? Who proclaimed it here,*
> *Whence, whence this manifold creation sprang?*
> *The Gods themselves came later into being...*
>
> *The Most High Seer that is in highest heaven,*
> *He knows it - or perchance e'en He knows not...*
>
> *Ere the foundations of the earth were laid...*
> *Thou wert. And when the subterranean flame*
> *Shall burst its prison and devour the frame...*
> *Thou shalt be still as Thou wert before*
> *And knew no change, when time shall be no more.*
> *Oh! endless thought, divine ETERNITY.'*

The Theosophical Society was founded in 1875 by Colonel Henry Steel Olcott and Madame Blavatsky, supported by William Quan Judge and several others. Its purposes were to revive the wisdom tradition of the ancients, to counteract widespread materialism, and help each human being to discover his or her true and eternal Higher Self again, gaining experience through all forms of manifestation during many reincarnations and guided by the Universal Law of Karma.

But karma neither punishes nor rewards, it is simply the one unerring Universal Law of Cause and Effect, guiding the evolution of the universe, nature, and man.

*The Secret Doctrine* reminds us that 'we stand bewildered before the mystery of our own making, and the riddles of life that *we will not* solve... But verily there is not an accident in our lives, not a misshapen day, or a misfortune, that could not be traced back to our own doings in this or in another life... The Law of Karma is inextricably interwoven with that of Reincarnation... It is only this doctrine, we say, that can explain to us the mysterious problem of Good and Evil, and reconcile man to the terrible *apparent* injustice of life. Nothing but such certainty can quiet our revolted sense of justice. For, when one unacquainted with the noble doctrine looks around him, and observes the inequalities of birth and fortune, of intellect and capacities; when one sees honour paid to fools and profligates, on whom fortune has heaped her favours by mere privilege of birth, and their nearest neighbour, with all his intellect and noble virtues - far more deserving in every way - perishing for want and for lack of sympathy; when one sees all this and has to turn away, helpless to relieve the undeserved suffering, one's ears ringing and heart aching with the cries of pain around him - that blessed knowledge of Karma alone prevents him from cursing life and men, as well as their supposed Creator...

'This law - whether Conscious or Unconscious - predestines nothing and no one. It exists from and in Eternity, truly, for it is Eternity itself; and as such ... it cannot be said to act, for it is Action itself... Karma creates nothing, nor does it design. It is man who plans and creates causes, and Karmic Law adjusts the effects, which adjustment is not an act, but universal harmony, tending ever to resume its original position... Karma has never sought to destroy intellectual and individual liberty, like the god invented by the Monotheists... Karma is an Absolute and Eternal Law in the World of Manifestation; and as there can only be one Absolute, as One eternal ever-present Cause, believers in Karma cannot be regarded as Atheists or Materialists - still less as Fatalists, for Karma is one with the Unknowable, of which it is an aspect, in its effects in the phenomenal world.'

It was the great Alexandrian philosopher Ammonius Saccas (175 AD -242 AD), the founder of the Neoplatonic school of the Philalethians or 'Lovers of Truth', who coined the term 'theosophy' for divine wisdom. Born of Christian parents, he honoured what was good in Christianity, but broke with the churches and dogmatism early in life, unable to find any superiority over older religions. He recognised that 'Theosophia' is 'the substratum and basis of all world religions and philosophies, taught and practised by a few elect ever since man became a thinking being.'[2] In its practical terms, theosophy is pure 'divine ethics'.[3] According to

Madame Blavatsky, it is: '... the occult hygiene of mind and body, the un-learning of false beliefs and the acquisition of true habits of thought' by its students.[4]

*The Voice of the Silence* is composed of three sections or Fragments. The following quotes from Fragment I may serve as guidance:

'Desire nothing. Chafe not at Karma, nor at Nature's changeless laws. But struggle only with the personal, the transitory, the evanescent and the perishable.

'Help Nature and work on with her; and Nature will regard thee as one of her creators and make obeisance.

'And she will open wide before thee the portals of her secret chambers, lay bare before thy gaze the treasures hidden in the very depths of her pure virgin bosom. Unsullied by the hand of matter she shows her treasures only to the eye of Spirit - the eye which never closes, the eye for which there is no veil in all her kingdoms.'

Fragment II contains the following insights:

'False learning is rejected by the Wise, and scattered to the Winds by the good Law. Its wheel revolves for all, the humble and the proud.

'The 'Doctrine of the Eye' is for the crowd, the 'Doctrine of the Heart' for the elect. The first repeat in pride: 'Behold, I know,' the last, they who in humbleness have garnered, low confess, 'thus have I heard'.

'The Dharma[5] of the 'Eye' is the embodiment of the external, and the non-existing.

'The Dharma of the 'Heart' is the embodiment of Bodhi,[6] the Permanent and Everlasting.

'... 'The branches of a tree are shaken by the wind; the trunk remains unmoved.'

'...Be humble, if thou would'st attain to Wisdom.

'Be humbler still, when Wisdom thou hast mastered.'

\* \* \*

Gottfried de Purucker was a scholar in ancient languages and leader of the Theosophical Society Pasadena from 1929 to 1942. In the first chapter of *The Book of the Golden Precepts*, 'The Path to the Heart of the Universe', he writes:

'There is a hunger in every human heart, which nothing can satisfy or appease... a hunger for the real, a hunger for the sublime. It is the nostalgia of the soul, of the spirit-soul of man. The source of this longing is the homesickness brought about by the soul-memory of our spiritual abode, whence we came and towards which we are now on our return journey.

'Men unconsciously, intuitively, unknown to the brain-mind, see the vision sublime on the mountain tops of the mystic East; and oh! this yearning homesickness for the indescribable, for the immortal, for the deathless, for that which brings unutterable peace and love which is frontierless in its reaches! Every human heart feels this, and it is the saving power in men, the thing which gives them hope and aspiration, which raises their souls with the recognition of the glory that once was theirs...

'There is a path, a sublime pathway of wisdom and illumination which begins, for each human being, in any one incarnation on this earth in the present life, and thereafter leads inward, for it is the pathway of conscious and spiritual realization leading ever inward, more inward, still more inward, toward the mystic East, which is the heart of the universe...

'This path to the universe is one and yet different for every human being. The meaning is that every human being himself is that pathway - that pathway which is builded of thought and consciousness, and of the fabric of your own being. It is builded of the stuff of Nature's heart... Man is an inseparable part of the universe in which he lives, moves and has his being... The same universal life flows through all things that are. The same stream of consciousness which flows... through the mighty Whole of the universe, flows therefore through man, an inseparable portion of that universe... There is a pathway by which you may come into intimate relation with the heart of the universe itself; and that pathway is you, your own inner being, your own inner nature, your spiritual self. Not the self of ordinary physical man, which self is just a poor reflection of the spiritual brilliance within, but that inner self of pure consciousness, pure love for all that is, unstained by any earthly taint - your spiritual being. 'Following this pathway to your own inner god, your higher self, you will reach all the mysteries and wonders of boundless infinitude, through infinite time; and such happiness and peace and bliss and beauty and love and inspiration will fill your whole being that every breath will be a blessing, and every thought a sublime inspiration.'

\* \* \*

The first object of the Theosophical Society is to form a nucleus of universal brotherhood of humanity without distinction of race, creed, gender, caste or colour, based on the eternal laws of the universe. According to *The Secret Doctrine*, these laws are present in every true religion and philosophy: 'The Secret Doctrine is the accumulated Wisdom of the Ages… But such is the mysterious power of Occult symbolism, that the facts which have actually occupied countless generations of initiated seers and prophets… are all recorded on a few pages of geometrical signs and glyphs…The system in question is no fancy of one or several isolated individuals… it is an uninterrupted record, covering thousands of generations of seers, whose respective experiences were made to test and verify the traditions, passed on orally by one early race to another... by men who have developed and perfected their physical, mental, psychic, and spiritual organisations, to the utmost possible degree...

'No vision of one Adept was accepted until it was checked and confirmed by the visions - so obtained as to stand as independent evidence - of other Adepts, and by centuries of experiences.'

In *Collected Writings Volume IX*, Blavatsky writes, 'On the day when Theosophy will have accomplished its most holy and most important mission - namely, to unite firmly a body of men of all nations in brotherly love and bent on a pure altruistic work, not on a labour with selfish motives - on that day only will Theosophy become higher than any nominal brotherhood of man. This will be a wonder and a miracle truly, for the realization of which Humanity is vainly waiting for the last 18 centuries, and which every association has hitherto failed to accomplish.'

'The term 'Universal Brotherhood' is no idle phrase', says the Mahatma Koot Hoomi[7] in the *The Mahatma Letters to Mr. A.P. Sinnett*, which were written during the early stages of the theosophical movement, and which can be viewed now in the British Library. 'Humanity in the mass has a paramount claim upon us,' he says ... 'It is the only secure foundation for universal morality. If it be a dream, it is at least a noble one for mankind: and it is the aspiration of the *true adept*.'

\* \* \*

Investigations in atomic and subatomic physics have revealed the illusory nature of matter. This has led many of today's scientists to express an increasingly mystical worldview. For example, Fritjof Capra, an Austrian-born theoretical physicist, suggests there are important similarities between the ways of the physicist and the mystic. In an article called 'Science and Spirituality' and in his book *Uncommon Wisdom,* he points out that scientific and mystical observations both take place in realms that are inaccessible to the ordinary senses.

In modern physics, these are the realms of the atomic and subatomic world. In mysticism, they are non-ordinary states of consciousness, in which the everyday sensory world is transcended. In both cases, access to these non-ordinary levels of experience is possible only after long years of training within a rigorous discipline, and in both fields the 'experts' assert that their observations often defy expressions in ordinary language.

It should, therefore, come as no surprise that the similarities between the worldviews of physicists and Eastern mystics are relevant not only to physics, but to science as a whole. Dr. Capra writes, 'If physics leads us today to a world view which is essentially mystical, it returns, in a way, to its beginning... This time, however, it is not only based on intuition, but also on experiments of great precision and sophistication, and on a rigorous and consistent mathematical formalism.'[8]

\* \* \*

Strong support for reincarnation also comes from Stuart Hameroff, Professor of Anaesthesiology at the University of Arizona, who teamed up in the 1990s with Sir Roger Penrose, Professor of Mathematics at Oxford University. In a united effort, they were trying to shed light on the mystery of consciousness, how it comes about, and its means of transmission.

We all know what it is like to be conscious or have awareness, but what is this conscious 'mind'? They asked themselves, how can the subjective nature of our phenomenal experiences - or our inner life - be explained in scientific terms?

The universe is perfectly tuned. The physical parameters (or measurable aspects of a system) determining physics, chemistry and biology (like the mass of a proton, the charge of an electron etc.) are precisely what they need to be to produce stars, light, life and consciousness. If any of these parameters were even slightly different, we would not exist.

Traditional religious systems suggest that God produced the physical parameters as they are. Some modern scientists take the view that there must be an infinite number of parallel universes (or the multiverse) and that we just happen to be in one of them that supports consciousness. This is the so-called Anthropic Principle.

Meanwhile, another very interesting theory has emerged. Sir Roger Penrose has suggested that the universe is serial rather than parallel. One universe follows another in an overall evolutionary scheme. The Big Bang was preceded by a previous universe, and that by another, in a series of universes developing in a serial evolutionary process. But what is the universe evolving towards? Together, Penrose and Hameroff developed a theory called 'Orchestrated Objective Reduction' (Orch OR), which is based on the following assumptions.

Consciousness is a process intrinsic to the fine scale structure of physical reality. It is inherent in space/time geometry at the Planck scale.[9] The theory is that there is information beyond the Planck scale, in a subjective realm, where the physical parameters of the universe are embedded and determined. The obvious implication of this theory is that, with each Big Bang and rebirth of the universe, the physical parameters change or mutate in an evolutionary process. The universe evolves to optimise consciousness.

According to *The Secret Doctrine*: '...Nature runs down and disappears from the objective plane, only to re-emerge after a time of rest out of the subjective, and to re-ascend once more. Our Kosmos and Nature will run down only to re-appear on a more perfect plane after every Pralaya.'[10]

Hameroff and Penrose's hypothesis suggests that consciousness is intrinsic, woven into the fabric of the universe. This is reflected in many spiritual and contemplative traditions and is a view shared by some scientists and philosophers. The implication is that conscious precursors and Platonic forms (as well as ethical values) precede biology and are extant in the fine scale structure of physical reality. It is consciousness that drives the universe.

Hameroff compares this idea of a conscious universe with what Hindu philosophy calls 'Brahma(n)', the essence of an omnipresent and aware universe; in that case, Atma would be an individualised ripple of that consciousness, 'spirit in the fabric of space and time', coalescing in a particular region within this underlying fabric of the universe, the container of all potentialities. It would suggest that there is an inner connectedness among human beings and the essence of the universe, a field of quantum vibrations containing platonic values or ethics, which humans can access as a kind of divine guidance. The quantum vibrations of consciousness would be more like music than computation (or mathematical calculations).

Penrose and Hameroff theorise that the physical medium in which consciousness occurs in the brain consists of microtubules. Microtubules are the largest filaments in the brain's neurons. They are hollow tubes, around which globular protein subunits called 'tubulins' are symmetrically arranged. Penrose and Hameroff propose that aspects of quantum theory, like the phenomenon of wave function 'self-collapse',[11] are essential for consciousness to occur. The particular characteristics of microtubules conducive to such quantum effects include their crystal-like lattice structure.

The brainwaves of a conscious person occur at a frequency of between 80 and 100 megahertz (MHz). Under an anaesthetic, brainwave activity drops to a range of 40 - 60 MHz. Lower frequencies are a sign of brain damage. When the brain function of a dying person is monitored, brainwave frequency drops to 0 as the heart stops beating. Then something extraordinary and anomalous happens. Brain activity reoccurs suddenly up to a frequency of 90 MHz for a period lasting between 90 seconds and 20 minutes. This phenomenon has been observed in patients who are brain-dead, and in animals. One could say that death seems to be the most awake moment.

These effects could be interpreted as the soul leaving the body. Many reports of near death experiences describe this as a time when the person re-lives all the stages of her or his life, as if watching a film. These phenomena seem to support the argument for an eternal soul.

The soul is an individualised unit of the very fabric of the universe itself. It acts as a quantum container of stored information about a person's life experiences. It can exist outside the body, or in other words, it can 'survive the death of the body' as a kind of entangled quantum soul with the accumulated experiences and latent possibilities necessary for further evolution. And if it is able to re-attach itself to its original body after an 'out-of-body' experience, why shouldn't it be able to attach itself to a new body - to reincarnate - as part of an evolutionary process, optimising its conscious awareness in order to fulfil its spiritual destiny?

\* \* \*

In *Self Knowledge*, H. P. Blavatsky reminds us that: 'The first necessity for obtaining self-knowledge is to become profoundly conscious of ignorance; to feel with every fibre of the heart that one is ceaselessly self-deceived.

'The second requisite is the still deeper conviction that such knowledge - such intuitive and certain knowledge - can be obtained by effort.

'The third and most important is an indomitable determination to obtain and face that knowledge. Self-knowledge of this kind is unattainable by what men usually call 'self-analysis'. It is not reached by reasoning or any brain process; for it is the awakening to consciousness of the Divine nature of man. To obtain this knowledge is a greater achievement than to command the elements or to know the future.'[12]

1. Mahayana or 'Great Vehicle' is the larger of the two main branches of Buddhism (the other is Theravada). Yogachara, literally 'yoga practice' emphasises the development of cognition, perception, and consciousness through the interior lens of meditation and other yogic practices.

2. Helena Petrovna Blavatsky, *The Theosophical Glossary*, The Theosophical Publishing Society, London, 1892.

3. Ibid.

4. Helena Petrovna Blavatsky, *Collected Writings Vol X*, Quest Books, Wheaton, Il. USA, 1966.

5. In Buddhism, dharma means 'cosmic law and order'.

6. The English term 'enlightenment' is the western translation of the abstract noun 'bodhi', the knowledge or wisdom, or awakened intellect, of a Buddha.

7. Koot Hoomi (also spelled Kuthumi, and frequently referred to simply as K.H.) is one of the Mahatmas that inspired the founding of the Theosophical Society in 1875. He engaged in a correspondence with two English theosophists living in India, A. P. Sinnett and A. O. Hume, which correspondence was published in the book *The Mahatma Letters to A. P. Sinnett*.

8. Fritjof Capra, *The Tao of Physics: An Exploration of the Parallels Between Modern Physics and Eastern Mysticism*, Shambhala Publications, 1975.

9. Planck scale refers to the magnitudes of space, time, energy and other units, below which (or beyond which) the predictions of the Standard Model of particle physics, quantum field theory and general relativity cannot be reconciled.

10. Pralaya is a Sanskrit word that means 'dissolution' or 'melting away' (from laya: 'to dissolve' and pra 'away'). In Hinduism, it refers to a period where the universe is in a state of non-

existence, which happens when the three gunas or qualities of matter are in perfect balance. H. P. Blavatsky defined it as, 'A period of obscuration or repose - planetary, cosmic or universal - the opposite of Manvantara.'

11. In quantum mechanics, wave function collapse occurs when a wave function - initially in a superposition of several eigenstates - reduces to a single eigenstate due to interaction with the external world. The word "eigenstate" is derived from the German/Dutch word 'eigen', meaning 'inherent' or 'characteristic'. An eigenstate is the measured state of some object possessing quantifiable characteristics such as position, momentum, etc. The state being measured and described must be observable (i.e. something such as position or momentum that can be experimentally measured either directly or indirectly), and must have a definite value, called an eigenvalue.

12. Helena Petrovna Blavatsky, *Self Knowledge*, Lucifer Vol 1, No. 2, George Redway, 1887.

Patience Sinnett

Patience Edensor Sinnett was an English theosophist who knew H. P. Blavatsky in the earliest days of the Theosophical Society in India. She was present with Blavatsky and others at the studio of the young German artist Hermann Schmiechen when he attempted to paint portraits of the Mahatmas Morya and Koot Hoomi.

She was born in 1844 to Richard and Clarissa Edensor in Sherston, Derbyshire, England. She married Alfred Percy Sinnett on 6 April 1870 at St. John's parish church in Notting Hill, London. In his autobiography, Sinnett described how she 'studied astrology profoundly'.

In 1872, George Allen, the proprietor of the Anglo-Indian newspaper, *The Pioneer*, offered Alfred Percy Sinnett the editorship. The couple moved to India where they lived until 1883.

On 16 May 1877, they had a son, Percy Edensor Sinnett, better known as 'Dennie'. His health was fragile throughout his rather short life. In March 1881, the family went to England for a holiday. Alfred returned to India but Patience, who was expecting her second child, remained in Notting Hill with her mother. On 14 July the baby was delivered still-born. She returned to India on 10 January 1882.

On 11 February 1883, the Sinnetts left Allahabad to return to England, where Patience would spend the rest of her life.

Dennie died of tuberculosis on 11 May 1908, at the age of 31. Patience died of cancer the same year at midnight on 9 November, despite her husband's efforts at mesmeric healing.

Patience Sinnett wrote two pamphlets in the Adyar Pamphlets series, number 193 and 194, entitled *The Purpose of Theosophy*. Henry Steel Olcott described them as 'an introductory manual for beginners'.

# The Purpose of Theosophy
## by Patience Sinnett (1885)

## Elementary Truths

Theosophy is not a religion with a creed or code of doctrines to which its followers must subscribe before they enter the fold. An erroneous belief that it is in this way a specific faith has, perhaps, taken hold of the public mind in the Western world - so far as the subject has obtained attention at all during the last few years - and the aim of the present explanation is to show what the general character and tendencies of theosophic thought really are; to point out in a concise and simple manner what it is that the study of Theosophy teaches and embraces, as well as what effect the reception of the knowledge to which it leads should have on the lives, work, and intercourse with their neighbours, and humanity at large, of those who try to benefit by and conform to it. Few will deny that for many years past, the tendency of intellectual thought and scientific inquiry has been towards Materialism and Agnosticism. Theology has become discredited by reason of having had for its supporters and preachers men who, instead of devoting themselves to the study or science of spirituality, have contented themselves with repeating, parrot-like in many cases, the phrases of those who have gone before; these phrases having been oftener than not originally formulated in order to make their acceptation by so-called heretics at the same time more difficult and more binding, and not for any real value or spiritual truth to be discovered in them. In other words, they have clung to the dogmas of their creeds instead of to the spirit of the teaching contained in the words of their various leaders. In spite, however, of this intellectual bias in favour of Materialism, there still remains in human nature the desire for belief in a future life; and the following pages aim at pointing out how the study of Theosophy, or, as it may be equally well called, the Esoteric Doctrine, among other things, shows the reason of this instinctive longing, and what it will necessarily and surely lead to in the future races of mankind.

As Theosophy is not in itself a religion in the common acceptation of the word, hardly even a philosophy, it may and does include among its followers representatives of almost every form of religious belief in the world, as well as many who have no belief at all. It teaches people to search for the fundamental truth that is the basis equally of every creed, philosophy, and science, to discover and put aside the superstructure raised by the superstition, persecution, love of power, ignorance of science, and bigotry of humanity, and thus to lay bare the fact that one truth supports every religion, no matter how divergent they may now appear; that truth being the Divine wisdom of the ancients, discoverable alike in the symbolical writings of the Kabbala, the Books of Hermes, the Vedas, and other sacred books of the East, in the Talmud, our own Bible, as well as the teachings of Pythagoras, Socrates, and many of the more recent philosophers. This Wisdom Religion, which is the germ of truth to be found in every form of belief worthy of the name, existed on this planet thousands of years before any of the creeds of Christendom were heard of, before the still more ancient religions of the East were recorded. In support of this last statement it may be explained that the Vedas, said to constitute the oldest book extant, were, for centuries before they were committed to writing, handed down orally from priest to priest, the real knowledge which was to be found in the teaching being considered of too sacred a character to entrust to any but those who have devoted their lives to the pursuit of this mystical wisdom. And to this day the real meaning of these books cannot be understood from the mere reading of them, even by the best Hindu Sanskrit scholars, inasmuch as by the intonation and variation of the voice an entirely different interpretation is given to the written words. Consequently a student of occultism, desiring to acquire the hidden knowledge that these books undoubtedly contain, must have them recited to him by his Guru (master), who by degrees, as the pupil advances, explains the true interpretation of the symbology.

The searcher for truth will find that Theosophy holds within its grasp an inexhaustible source of knowledge in every groove of thought, whether on the spiritual or physical plane. There is no science, no art, no intellectual pursuit, in whatever direction it may incline, that Theosophy, as now understood, does not embrace and pervade: its study cannot but render wiser and more elevated every human creature.

One of the first truths for a student to realise

is that of reincarnation, or spirit-evolution. A belief in this doctrine may be found to permeate nearly all ancient philosophies; and it recommends itself to the thoughtful mind by accounting satisfactorily for the inequalities in life to be observed everywhere around us, both in the animal and human kingdoms. How is it possible, otherwise, to reconcile the apparent injustice of one man being born in absolute misery and want, in a position where improvement, or even the desire for improvement, is impossible; while another, no more deserving, as far as can be seen, is surrounded by friends, luxuries, and everything that can make life desirable? Why are we to accept the theory of evolution up to a certain point, and then cast it off abruptly, saying, this is the end, here all progress ceases? Is it not more reasonable to suppose, arguing from analogy, that Nature, having by a long course of evolution through the many and various forms of the inferior kingdoms, developed the humanity of which we now have cognisance, proceeds from this point onward with an infinite hope of spiritual and psychical advancement, which is now only beginning to be dimly perceived as possible, but which, in the course of time, will become an accepted fact; accepted because, instead of, as now, the psychical faculties being of rare and most exceptional occurrence, they may then be the appanage[1] of the majority?

But it is not necessary here to argue in favour of, or against, this doctrine; it is enough to show, very briefly, that it has to come into the scheme of theosophic teaching. The reader, however, must not imagine that by reincarnation is meant the transmigration of human souls into the bodies of animals, for this could hardly be called spiritual progress. What has ever to be kept in mind is the gradual but sure ascent of every thing upon this globe, from the mineral and vegetable up to man, and from man up to God. But it must not be thought that by this word is meant the Anthropomorphic, or personal God of orthodox Christianity. It is used here as the only available term adapted to express what is variously described as the 'Absolute Power', 'Supreme Unity', 'Ultimate Reality', 'Divine Spirit', etc. which pervades all space, and of which the manifestation may be found in every thing around us, both animate and inanimate.

It is the awakening of this Divine Spirit within us that gives rise, in some cases, to a feeling of certainty of a future state, in others to an indescribable longing that it should be so; it is this something belonging to, but independent of, the body, that endows earnest Christians, or followers of any other religion, no matter of what age or country, with the hope and assurance of heavenly happiness after death.

On this doctrine of reincarnation depends that no less important one of Karma - the law of cause and effect operating through the merit and demerit of a person's deeds in each life.

Every individual is making Karma either good or bad in each action and thought of his daily round, and is at the same time working out in this life the Karma brought about by the acts and desires of the last. But it must be remembered that the ego, the real man, the individuality, has no spiritual origin in the parentage by which it is reembodied, but is drawn by the affinities which its previous mode of life attracted round it, into the current that carries it, when the time comes for re-birth, to the home best fitted for the development of those tendencies. And here it may be remarked, that the human race *en gros*, is improving and evolving to a much higher state of development than we at present - in consequence of our great materiality - can realise.

This doctrine of Karma when properly understood is well calculated to guide and assist those who realise its truth, to a higher and better mode of life, for it must not be forgotten that not only our actions but our thoughts also are most assuredly followed by a crowd of circumstances that will influence for good or for evil our own future, and what is still more important, the future of many of our fellow creatures. If sins of omission and commission could in any case be only self-regarding, the effect on the sinner's Karma would be a matter of minor consequence. The fact that every thought and act through life carries with it for good or evil a corresponding influence on other members of the human family, renders a strict sense of justice, morality, and unselfishness so necessary to future happiness and progress. A crime once committed, an evil thought sent out from the mind, are past recall - no amount of repentance can wipe out their results in the future. 'Can the *results* of a crime be obliterated even though the crime itself should be pardoned? The effects of a cause are never limited to the boundaries of the cause, nor can the results of crime be confined to the offender and his victim. Every good as well as evil action has its effects, as palpably as the stone flung into a calm water.'[2] Repentance, if sincere, will deter a man from repeating errors; it cannot save him or others from the effects of those already produced, which will most unerringly overtake him either in this life or in the next re-birth.

If men and women kept the law of Karma well in minds shaping their lives in conformity with it, they would not have so much to answer for in regard to harm done to their neighbours. But the ethics of this teaching show that active good is required of its followers as well as abstention from evil; and one of the grandest lessons taught by Theosophy is that of universal brotherhood, which rightly interpreted means a large-hearted desire to benefit humanity. Almost every person, no matter how humble, can in one way or another help to comfort by words or deeds some of his fellow creatures. How much more, therefore, lies in the power of the educated classes? - and it is to the latter that these words are addressed. Philanthropy is open to them on two planes - the physical and spiritual, for they are able both to act and to think; and this philosophy teaches that thoughts may even in some cases be of more importance than actions, inasmuch as the latter, being on the material plane, affect only physical lives in future incarnations, while the former, belonging to the higher plane, have consequences even more far-reaching, that affect the spiritual and therefore real existence.

The Karma made by our actions and general tendencies decides our future incarnations on this planet; Karma due to intellectual work and thoughts affects more directly our spiritual condition hereafter, determining the duration and character of heavenly bliss, previous to re-birth on the material plane. Thus, as we pass along our earthly lives, we leave behind us a train of events which no after-repentance can obliterate, which must with absolute certainty bring about their inevitable results in the next re-birth. All the varying states of happiness and the reverse, are due, not to the caprice of a single birth and life, but are the direct consequences of previous tendencies or actions committed by the individual.

This in bare outline is the great law of Karma. There are, of course, details and side-issues innumerable, which it would be out of place to enter upon in an elementary work of this nature. The reader once interested in the philosophy can gather for himself fuller information from the many books now obtainable that deal with these subjects.

## Outline of Occult History

As already stated, the Divine wisdom of the ancients has been the basis and essence of all great popular religions. The unwholesome growths fed by time and human passions that now overrun them, when brushed away, display underneath, the true revelation still uninjured and untouched.

What does this Divine wisdom really consist of, whence comes it, by whom has it been taught, and for what purpose?

In looking back along the records of the past, it may be observed that the educated members of society have always been in possession of knowledge the diffusion of which among the multitude was thought to be undesirable. In quite the most distant times of which history can give us any information, the highest and, from the present standpoint, the only class with any erudite culture was to be found among those who had been initiated in arcane knowledge by the hierophants of the mysteries. 'Every nation had its mysteries and hierophants... who alone could impart the awful knowledge contained in the Merkaba.'[3] Those who had in their keeping this sacred religion were magicians, the word coming from 'Mage', or 'Magian'; magic being in those days considered, as in truth it was and still is, a Divine science, its study leading to the discovery of the hidden workings of nature, by the cultivation of the spiritual qualities inherent in man. For, in order to attain, while in the body, the state necessary for the perception and apprehension of these invisible operations, the initiate must have led a life of absolute purity in all respects - in actions, thoughts, motives, aspirations, and desires. It was not the sacerdotal classes in Persia who discovered magic, as some might imagine from the word.

Those were called 'magi' who became learned in this science.

The study of ancient occult writings discloses the fact that the knowledge and practice of magic has been in the world since the earliest races of man. The following quotation from *Isis Unveiled* may help to assure the reader on these points: 'What we desire to prove is, that underlying every ancient popular religion was the same ancient wisdom-doctrine, one and identical, professed and practised by the initiates of every country, who alone were aware of its existence and importance. To ascertain its origin and the precise way in which it was matured is now beyond human possibility. A single glance, however, is enough to assure one that it could not have attained the marvellous perfection in which we find it pictured to us in the relics of various esoteric systems except after a succession of ages. A philosophy so profound, a moral code so ennobling, and practical results so conclusive and so uniformly demonstrable, cannot be the growth of a generation or even of a single epoch. Fact must have been piled upon fact, deduction on deduction, science has begotten science, and generations upon generations of the brightest human intellects have reflected on the laws of nature, before this ancient doctrine had taken concrete shape. The proofs of this identity of fundamental doctrine in the old religions are found in the prevalence of a system of initiation in the sacerdotal castes which had the guardianship of mystical words of power, and a public display of phenomenal control over natural forces indicating association with preter-human beings. Every approach to the mysteries of all these nations was guarded with the same jealous care, and in all the penalty of death was inflicted upon initiates of any degree who divulged the secrets entrusted to them... Such was the case in the Eleusinian and Bacchic mysteries, among the Chaldean magi and the Egyptian hierophants, while with the Hindus, from whom they were all derived, the same rule has prevailed from time immemorial.'

Again, 'The mysteries are as old as the world, and one well versed in the esoteric mythologies of various nations can trace them back to the days of the ante-Vedic period in India.'

Thus it will be seen that the knowledge and practice of occult science may be traced back in the past as far as historical records extend, and in each successive generation the followers of, and practical workers in, these studies, have always been found among the most brilliant scholars of the day. But notwithstanding that at one period occult research brought in its train persecution, tortures and death, it carried with it such an ardent desire for further knowledge, that no fear of consequences could prevent the pursuit of it when once entered upon by educated men. And it is only fair to assume that something more than theoretical results must have urged on those who risked their lives and reputations in devotion to this superstition, as it is vulgarly called.

The inmost secrets of the science, however, have been retained and scrupulously guarded from the profane by devoted custodians, who have exercised the powers within their grasp only for the advancement of the races, both materially and spiritually, as necessity arose, or the state of humanity allowed. In far distant ages the people on their part regarded these guardians with absolute devotion and reverence, abiding by their laws in simple faith.

From the great root of this science have shot out in various directions, sometimes underground and often unnoticed, branches and tendrils of less and less virtue and power as they wandered further and further away from the original stem, but ever kept alive and continually breaking out afresh into activity owing to their connection with the far distant source of life. Alchemy, astrology, witchcraft, demonology, sorcery, spiritualism and every other name and form of what is commonly called the supernatural, spring from and owe their existence to the esoteric doctrine of the Ancients. The same order of events may be observed in regard to the various phases of occult history as in those of religious history - the same substratum of truth, the gradual separation of groups of people following individual leaders, these in their turn dividing again, each successive rupture carrying the members further away from the truth, until at last it is with the greatest difficulty that the slight thread of resemblance can be perceived that shows the bond of union between these errant sects and their original point of departure.

But it may be asked, how can a sacred science

of such enormous pre-eminence as is claimed for this one - the avenues to which are, and always have been, guarded with so much care, betrayal of knowledge acquired by an entrance into whose innermost mysteries was punishable by death - how does it happen, then, that in a community barricaded by such stringent rules, and so exceedingly difficult of access, deterioration could, even in the lapse of ages, ever take place? The answer is that deterioration of the real philosophy has not nor ever can set in, for the truths of these sublime mysteries can be given only to those who have, through years of study, preparation, and trial, proved themselves, beyond all doubt, worthy of them; and the fact that there are still custodians of these mysteries, and that initiation thereinto is the work of perhaps more than one or even two incarnations, shows that corruption, due to time and human desires, has not yet entered their community, nor sullied the purity of their work. At the same time, the position in the world held by these adepts in times gone by was one of immense power. They were the law-givers of their countries, and had entire control not only over the masses, but also over temporal rulers. In spite, therefore, of the austerities and rigour of life required for admittance into the ranks of studentship, numbers, it may easily be imagined, would strive to attain the knowledge that carried with it such inestimable advantages, even from the worldly point of view. Again, those who had by dint of asceticism gained some little insight into the way to work occult phenomena of the physical kind, but who had failed of the higher initiations through, perhaps, want of purity of motive, were tempted, probably, to carry into distant places the limited knowledge they had gathered in the course of their training, and were able with comparative ease to pass themselves off on the ignorant people as real adepts, using thus, for their own personal benefit and aggrandisement, what was only intended to be for the good and progress of humanity at large. False teachers such as these would attract round them pupils or followers who in their turn would be inferior to their masters, until at last the science would be lowered and degraded in public estimation. History shows that, even in the time of the old Egyptians, belief in the supernatural powers of the priests and oracles of the temples was, among the aristocracy, fast crumbling away, but the power and authority that the priests still maintained over the army and country at large was too great to be disregarded. The king and his courtiers went on fulfilling their public devotions for the sake of example, and to keep the favour of the priests, and not because they believed in the prophecies of the oracles or the so-called miracles performed at the religious rites and festivals. These may often have become too transparently fraudulent to deceive any but the most illiterate adherents. As long as the hierophants and priests of the temples were true adepts, i.e. had passed their initiations, and were consequently free from all worldly ambition - they had no need of resorting to the jugglery and imposture that eventually wore out the belief of the people and brought discredit upon the religion. But, in spite of this degradation of the science in general estimation, due in part to the lapse of time, and in part to some of the lower forms of its knowledge escaping and being misused, the highest initiation to adeptship has never been taken by any individual who was capable of bringing discredit on the brotherhood, or of divulging to any one of the sacred mysteries. None but the deified man could attain the requisite development; and, having reached this height, he would be far above any temptation that the attractions of this world could hold out.

Moreover, there are other roads leading to occult science besides that by which each pupil or chela, in turn, hopes to attain adeptship. Even these may not be easy to climb, and training, even for minor achievements, must be severe. But when, as occasionally may have been the case, the aim of the candidate has merely been the accomplishment of phenomena for worldly advantage or the desire for supremacy over his fellow creatures, these lower aims may have been secured with relative facility, and consequently by students of an ignoble type. The possession of powers by such persons would obviously tend to lower in the eyes of the world the science from which such powers spring. And this consideration gives another explanation of the way in which magic, as a source of power, has been turned from its intended use; and, instead of being recognised as a necessary attribute of real religion, the knowledge of which must be wielded for the benefit of society, has been discredited as a branch of study both from the pulpit and by the State - from the former as being forbidden by the Bible and an unholy pursuit, by the latter as being an exploded and mischievous belief that never had any foundation except in the minds of the ignorant and superstitious people of the olden time.

The history of the rise and fall of all religions may be traced to reasons almost identical in every nation, whether Eastern or Western. The craving for immortality which is inherent in humanity, is the feeling that has always influenced people to follow one or another of the religions that have appeared from time to time in the history of the world. These religions, so long as the teaching given by their respective leaders was upheld by their disciples or descendants, in its integrity - so long as no worldly prejudices nor selfish motives sullied the lives of the clergy or priests - would never have fallen into the state of decadence now only too apparent to their most fervent adherents. But when what ought to be regarded only as a vocation, the result of an overwhelming desire to help humanity to a perception of the spiritual in Nature, becomes a profession in which a struggle for pre-eminence is a matter of course, the effect on the religion will and must be the same. Whether that struggle takes the form of a desire for an enlarged sphere of action in the shape of a bishopric instead of a vicarage, or for priesthood in a large and popular temple as against an obscure and comparatively unknown one; gradually, but quite surely, doubts, disunions, separation, and disintegration follow in its train; until, as now, we see, both in the East and West, a large predominance of agnosticism and atheism. The majority of what are called Orthodox Christians are either those who have neither read nor thought at all on metaphysical subjects, or they are in truth, when their beliefs are dissected, esoteric Christians, with no firm attachment to the dogmas that go to make up and support the Church as it is now constituted.

The immediate disciples of Buddha, Jesus, or any of the other great religious reformers, were raised immeasurably above their contemporaries by contact with, belief in, and assurance of the absolute purity of motive, goodness, and entire unselfishness of their respective teachers, whose moral codes, miracles, and simple lives varied so little that it is hardly difficult for students to see that their knowledge must have been drawn from the same source, although they lived at very different periods of time.

The moral code taught and practised by Jesus, as far as it goes, is perfect and most ennobling. But even this has been compatible with persecution, bloodshed, torture, and immorality of every sort. Scientific research and material progress have been paralysed in the desperate struggle of the clergy to maintain their power and supremacy, gained and upheld by violence. From the few simple words of Jesus his followers have been able to build up not only the two vast divisions in Christendom of Protestantism and Catholicism, but also the innumerable sects to be found within their respective folds. In view of all this, it is not surprising, considering its much greater antiquity, that the wisdom-religion of the ancients should have been misrepresented and disguised in the course of successive generations.

Enough has now been said to show the reader or, at all events, to put him on the track of verifying for himself the fact that Eastern and Western religions, magic, and occultism, with all their various developments, have one and the same origin.

## Western Misconceptions of Eastern Philosophy

When European scholars first began to interest themselves in the translation of the sacred books of the East, it was with no idea that they contained any deep system of thought which, when correctly interpreted, would go far to explain many of the enigmas of life or that in their ancient pages would be found some of the profoundest cosmological truths - but rather in the pursuit of philological and historical science. Their value to the educated European world was supposed to lie in their great antiquity, and not in the thoughts and ideas contained in them, which were never supposed worth serious study as embodying a philosophy. In the June edition of *The Nineteenth Century*[4] of last year (the first edition of this manual for beginners was published in 1885), Professor Max Müller,[5] in the course of an article entitled 'Forgotten Bibles', makes the following remarks: 'Some at least of the most important works illustrating the ancient religions of the East have been permanently rescued from oblivion, and rendered accessible to every man who understands English. Some of my friends, men whose judgment I value far higher than my own, wonder what ground there is for rejoicing. Some, more honest than the rest, told me that they had been great admirers of ancient Oriental wisdom till they came to read the translations of the sacred books of the East. They had evidently expected to hear the songs of angels and not the babbling of babes. But others took higher ground. What, they asked, could the philosophers of the 19th Century expect to learn from the utterances of men who had lived one, two, three, or even four thousand years ago? When I humbly suggested that these books had a purely historical interest, and that the history of religion could be studied from no other documents, I was told it was perfectly known how religion arose, and through how many stages it had to pass in its development from fetishism to positivism, and that, whatever facts might be found in the sacred books of the East, they must all vanish before theories which are infallible and incontrovertible.'

These remarks illustrate forcibly the fact that the translators have only appreciated their subject from one point of view, viz, that of its antiquity, and it is obvious that the idea has not occurred to them that these books might have a hidden meaning, which has been wrapped up in a symbology only recognisable to those who have made a study of mystic philosophy. It was not, of course, to be expected that Western Orientalists, or even Orientals educated exclusively in the Western school, should be able to interpret the symbology, but they should have been prepared to accept the possibility of its presence in the documents. These books may, perhaps, have been 'rescued from oblivion' by their present translators in regard to the English-speaking public at large; but an earnest inquirer, anxious to fathom the depth of Oriental thought, has even now, with these translations so readily available, to seek an interpretation of their veiled as well as their superficial meaning. Their 'rescue' has only been accomplished at the expense of their significance. These books have very much more than a mere historical value, for in their pages are to be found the fundamental truths of a philosophy that is received by many cultured minds as one well worthy of respect on quite other grounds than those of antiquity.

With reference to the Rig Veda, with which Max Müller claims so much familiarity, the following assertion, not unsupported by reason and illustration, is to be found in *Isis Unveiled:* 'Alchemists, kabalists, and students of mystic philosophy will find therein a perfectly defined system of evolution in the cosmogony of a people who lived a score of thousands of years before our own era. They will find in it, moreover, a perfect identity of thought, and even doctrine, with the Hermetic philosophy, and also that of Pythagoras and Plato.'

Apart from this, it might be asked what philosophers has the world to show in the present generation to compare with those who have passed away ages ago, leaving behind them theories which may perhaps come nearer the truth than those which are above referred to as 'infallible and incontrovertible'. The ideas to be found in the sacred books of the East are likened by the Professor to the 'babbling of babes'. Is this the fault of the ideas or is it not just possible to conceive that the translators, highly educated, painstaking and studious as they have shown themselves to be, have failed to find the mystical key that will unlock these hidden treasures, and without which these Bibles are comparatively meaningless and useless. Even from the historical point of view these translations must be unsatisfactory for, instead of helping to show the state of intellectual advancement of the people in those remote times, their actual knowledge of, or the theories they were capable of forming about, the Universe, they give (the learned mystics of India maintain) an entirely wrong impression to the reader of what those theories really were, and to what knowledge those who held them had attained. Justice cannot be done to the noble conceptions contained in these books in consequence of the spirit of the teaching being absolutely wanting in the English version. Were it possible to get these translations commented upon or annotated by an educated Brahmin, possessing some knowledge of the eastern doctrine, the whole philosophy would shine with a splendour which can now be only partially apprehended even by those Europeans who are disciples of eastern wisdom, and would display the true grandeur and intellectual power of its cosmogony. For, no matter to what sect the Brahmin might belong, whether he would give the reading in favour of one particular sect or another, it would not affect the result, for, as said above, Indian religions may and do differ considerably exoterically but the broad basis of esoteric identity is recognised by their respective cultured and mystical adherents and priests, and they one and all acknowledge the hidden occult meaning which underlies each of these writings, and which, in order to obtain their proper appreciation, must be perceived, if not believed in, by the translator.

Without this perception of the fact that occult science is the basis and foundation of all these books, no rendering of them will or can be satisfactory, for it should be the duty and wish of everyone engaged in the work of giving to others certain information by putting it from one language into another, first of all to be sure that he has got a true understanding of this author's subject otherwise how can he hope to do justice to the ideas, no matter how feeble and childish they may to him appear? Eastern philosophy has one great foundation of belief that runs through all the various forms of thought whether orthodox Brahminical, Buddhist, or Vedantist, and this resembles broadly what Mr. Draper[6] gives as that of the stoics or followers of Zeno:[7] 'Though there is a Supreme Power, there is no Supreme Being. There is an invisible principle, but not a personal God, to whom it would be not so much blasphemy as absurdity to impute the form, sentiments, the passions of men... That which we call chance is only the effect of an unknown cause. Even of chances there is a law. There is no such thing as Providence for nature proceeds under irresistible laws, and in this respect the Universe is only a vast automatic engine. The vital force which pervades the world is what the illiterate call God. The modifications through which all things are running take place in an irresistible way, and hence it may be said that the progress of the world is under destiny: like a seed it can evolve only in a predestined mode.'

The charge of Atheism so often brought against Theosophists and students of Eastern philosophy could hardly be more entirely baseless than it is, and would seem to owe its origin either to ignorance of the true work that Theosophists have at heart (viz. the suppression of Materialism) or to a wrong interpretation put upon the meaning of the word in its popular acceptation.

An Atheist is generally supposed to be one who not only does not believe in a God, but who is also convinced that there is for humanity no survival after death.

It would be equally just, and quite as logical to maintain that Spiritualists (who pass most of their spare time in holding communications with their friends and relations who have passed away) are Atheists, as that Buddhists and Theosophists are so. For, although these latter may disagree with some of the conclusions formed by the former as to the spiritual condition of the disembodied souls, they are at one in knowing that such communications are not only possible but of daily and hourly occurrence.

The one thing that a study of Theosophy shows more than another is that this life is as nothing compared to the next, that the present is but maya, i.e. transitory, whereas the real life is that which pertains to the inner man and which is apart from the body. While we are in the body we are chained down by it and are subject to the limitations incurred by its occupation. Freed from corporeal restraints we can take cognisance of existence on another and higher plane where time, distance, and death do not affect us. Buddhism teaches its disciples, among other things, to disregard the cravings of the body by subduing and conquering the desires that have to do with material pleasures, to be uninfluenced by feelings of envy, passion, anger, revenge, to cultivate an ardent wish to benefit humanity, combined with spiritual aspirations. These bodily desires, the lower feelings of our nature, being once destroyed, the inner man can then escape from bondage and gain while still in this life some of the knowledge and experience of another state of existence, and thereby of the reality of the ever progressing power of the Divine Spirit within, which likewise animates the whole universe. The mere fact that true Buddhism does not preach a belief in or dependence on a personal God is no proof that the religion is Atheistic, for it recognises in the Universal Spirit all the higher attributes which

Christianity assigns to its Deity while the teaching of Buddhism and of Christianity equally lead to the purification of the body from all worldly cares and ambition. The whole code of ethics as laid down by Jesus is to the end that humanity should be unselfish, so that their inner and spiritual selves may be fit to associate with the Father in Heaven. The Eastern teaching gives very much the same advice - crush and subdue the personality - that you may come to realise your oneness with the whole, universal consciousness.

The reader must not, however, suppose that Theosophy teaches Buddhism pure and simple, for this is not the case, but the study of it shows very clearly that the old wisdom-religion, as taught by initiates from time immemorial, underlies all the great religions of the world. Buddhism and Brahminism bear much the same relation one to another as do Protestantism and Catholicism, and they have as many sects and branches within their members as have these Western religions. Esoteric Buddhism was a philosophy before the historical Buddha appeared on the earth, that is to say, the philosophical truth beneath the outer form was there, as it was also in Christianity and Brahminism, before their founders appeared. Thus it will be seen that Oriental philosophy, instead of being atheistical in its tendency, is absolutely the reverse, and has got that character partly from being wrongly interpreted by Western exponents, and partly through the fact that a belief in an anthropomorphic God as the creator of the Universe is discouraged by the greatest Eastern authorities of the day, and is not supported in the teachings of the sacred books of the East.

Mr. Herbert Spencer's[8] 'Infinite and Eternal Energy from which all things proceed', and his statement that 'none of the positive attributes which have ever been predicated of God can be used of this energy', agrees and is identical with the teaching of Eastern philosophy. But, whereas Mr. Spencer says that human finite consciousness cannot conceive of, nor approach, the Unknowable, which he admits is the 'Ultimate Reality', occult initiates assert that the power to do so is latent in mankind, also that this power of faculty can, by special methods of development to the knowledge of which they have access, be brought to dominate and free itself from the restraints of the body and be rendered able to bridge the gulf that separates the known from the unknown. The deep reverence with which the teachers and pupils of the esoteric doctrine approach the subject of the Great Law - the Unconscious, Infinite, Ultimate Reality, or whatever name is used to express the idea - if only faintly realised by Western exponents of other religious beliefs, would go far to dispel the notion so widely circulated that this system is other than the most spiritual of all, for its great object is the cultivation in human beings of the higher tendencies of their nature thus enabling them to realise for themselves the great truth that this physical is the transitory and the spiritual the only real life.

## The Seen and Unseen

In order better to comprehend the connection which links the material to what is commonly called the spiritual world, it will be necessary for the reader to know that Eastern philosophy teaches the division of man into seven principles, which are as follows: 1. The Body; 2. Vitality; 3. Astral Body; 4. Animal

Soul; 5. Human Soul; 6. Spiritual Soul; 7. Spirit. In this division it will be seen that the body represents a gross form of matter, yet possesses the potentiality of spiritual development which is slowly brought to perfection by a long course of evolution through many incarnations. Yet it must not be supposed that these principles can be separated or torn one from the other like coats of skin or that they have distinct and individual properties that can work independently of one another. Each principle, on the contrary, is closely allied to its neighbour and can only work when thus supported. The body is of no use unless it is vitalised; the astral body would be, while away from its fleshly case, unintelligent, were it not illumined by the higher faculties of the animal soul, and the higher parts of the human soul itself would, at the death of the human being, cling to the astral form, and with that slowly disintegrate on the astral plane, but for their affinity and close adherence to the spiritual soul.

The first three principles belong exclusively to the personality and are perishable at the death of the body - i.e. the second principle, when no longer occupied with the body, goes to vitalise other organisms in its immediate vicinity while the astral form decays more slowly but as surely as does the body. The four higher principles form the individuality, the real inner man - the ego that passes from one incarnation to another. If, by a long course of deterioration due to a continued series of births of more and more debasing tendencies, the sixth and seventh principles become eventually detached from the higher portions of the fifth, the latter sinks and is merged in the fourth, which very slowly disintegrates in the astral light, during which time it is one of the most dangerous kind of elementaries.[9] The pure spirit which has thus been forced away from the ego flies back to its original source, the universal spirit. These principles are latent not only in animals down to the lowest organisms but also in all matter, whether organic or inorganic. Thus it may be said that a pebble contains the potential elements of the perfected man. This, however, does not mean that any particular stone will, in the course of millions of years, be converted into a man or that, although there is in it undoubtedly the latent germ of the life principle, therefore it will be ever able to move by its own volition. The theory of evolution, which agrees up to a certain point with occult science, maintains that the vegetable kingdom evolves from the mineral, the animal from the vegetable, and so on. It follows, therefore, that in the stone there must be the elements of the vegetable and animal, consequently of man, for it is hardly necessary here to consider the question of a separate creation for the human being.

The higher principles in man are developed in him, one by one, by slow degrees as he works his way up from primitive man up to the most advanced civilisations. Even in these the higher principles are still only latent. Most people at this present stage of humanity are only in active possession of their fourth principle, although the fifth is beginning to assert and manifest itself. This is shown in the development of the material intellect on the material plane, which deals almost entirely with subjects connected with the well-being of this life - scientific discovery, the education of the masses, historical research, and so on, tending for the most part towards disbelief in any other existence than the one, and consequently to the encouragement of bodily comfort and ease, rather than to the recognition of the spiritual and psychical powers in man, which are just beginning to unfold. When once these faculties are acknowledged, the way to their development and training discovered, all other sciences and studies will sink into relative neglect and become subject to the immense powers of the human will, the education of which will be the highest ambition of all those who have for their aim the attainment of real truth, or in other words, universal knowledge. This, however, will not be until humanity is in full possession of its fifth principle, glorified by the awakening of the sixth.

Even now, an educated minority is beginning to be aware that these higher faculties are innate in all and varyingly active in many. The separability in life of the astral from the material body has been proved beyond a doubt. Mesmerism, clairvoyance, magnetism, the passage of matter through matter, mental telegraphy, instantaneous transport of objects from distant places, are facts which may be tested and realised to be true by those who are sufficiently interested in these subjects to give the necessary time to such research, and who find themselves, without such proofs, unable to realise a future life or a conscious existence after death. The exceptional people who are born with, or who become possessed of, the abnormal powers, or spiritual capabilities which bring about the phenomena referred to above, may be roughly divided into two classes, those who from youth upward have been trained in a special manner with a view to the cultivation and expansion of their spiritual and psychical powers, and those who are naturally born seers and mediums, but who have grown up without any intelligent training specially directed to the cultivation of their peculiar gifts.

There is a broad difference between a seer and a medium although the two are connected by certain fundamental resemblances. The former possesses a far higher natural development than the latter and his powers are his own to wield as he pleases. The medium, as his name implies, is but a passive agent of communication between influences from the subjective or spiritual side of nature and ourselves. The bond of similarity which connects the two consists mainly in the fact that they can both be approached by, and have communication with, the inhabitants of the unseen world around us.

Mediums can, under certain conditions, get the physical phenomena with which almost every one is now familiar but cannot dictate what those conditions are to be, nor ever be quite sure that the results expected and hoped for will be forthcoming. The seer, on the other hand, by the concentration of his mind on a particular subject, can put himself *en rapport* with the spiritual plane and, while in a perfectly conscious and natural state, see into the astral light, not only exchanging ideas with the people therein but also reading with great accuracy the thoughts and intentions of those living in this world. These thoughts are photographed, more or less vividly, in the astral light according to the strength of the will that has projected them. In this way a murder has been distinctly seen by a clairvoyant, in all its details, weeks before it was committed, and the murderer identified by the seer, who recognised him at once, and unmistakably, from the picture he had seen in the astral light. Events such as this illustrate very clearly the great and lasting effect thoughts may have for good or evil on our fellow creatures. The steady intention of a murderer to commit a crime, which he carefully plans in all its minutiae, gets pictured in the astral light and only fades away after a longer or shorter lapse of time and it may, as long as it remains there, influence other people of evil tendencies to the commission of like crimes should they happen to come within reach of this particular current. They would not see the picture as does the clairvoyant, but the evil magnetism therefrom might enter their minds and develop the bad qualities lying dormant there, which otherwise would, perhaps, have never been aroused. The reader may here ask, what is this astral light into which a seer can look but which to the generality of people is a blank page - a name without a meaning.

The astral light is what in Sanskrit literature, is spoken of as Akasha. It is the store-house from whence the adept obtains, by will-force, the requisites for the working of phenomena of the creative kind. 'Akasha is the mysterious fluid termed by scholastic science 'the all-pervading ether'; it enters into all the magical operations of nature and produces mesmeric, magnetic, and spiritual phenomena... The word 'As', 'Ah', or 'Iah', means life-existence, and is evidently the root of the word akasha, which in Hindustan, is pronounced ahasha, the life-principle, or Divine life-giving fluid or medium.[10] This excessively attenuated fluid, or medium, which encompasses this world, pervades the universe, and surrounds everything in life, receives and records all our thoughts for a longer or shorter period, according to the intensity and precision with which they are conceived. It is in astral light that the slowly disintegrating souls of the dead, called by the teachers of Eastern philosophy, 'elementaries' may be seen. It is here, also, that elementals, sub-human beings, and the Deva kingdom must be looked for but until the higher principles of humanity are developed, either in the natural course of time, or by special training now, the astral light and all the secrets of nature therein contained must remain unknown to, and therefore unbelieved by, the majority. The ego of man cannot, while it is encased in the body as at present constituted, take cognizance of things on the spiritual plane but the study of theosophy, in one of its branches, teaches how to train and subdue the body into such a condition that the spiritual man within may be able to assert his powers and be in a great measure independent of it. The invisible world around is infinitely more various and interesting than the one which we know, not because it is unseen, but because it is more real, more lasting, more spiritual, and, above all, because in it is to be found the clue and sequel to so much that is a puzzle and mystery in regard to man's existence on this planet.

In science we are continually being told that such things are 'facts', 'laws of nature', and can only be accounted for by the vaguest conjectures. All the patient research of our most able men, for years and years past, has brought us no nearer to their solution. The attractive and repellant poles of the magnet, the recurrence and regular variations of the tide, and electric action, are 'facts' but how are they accounted for except by theories all more or less unsatisfactory. It must not be supposed, however, that all these problems will be solved at death, nor that the mere power in itself of being able to look into the astral light, or, in other words, being *en rapport*, while in the body, with a different plane of matter, will clear up all the difficulties pertaining to the two states of existence, for assuredly this is not the case. What it is desirable for a student to comprehend is, that a conviction as to the existence of the invisible world and its close connection with the visible is one step in the direction of real knowledge, and the next is a belief in the necessity of these spiritual powers, latent in man, being brought to a high state of development. The process of such development carries with it a comprehensive study of the working of the great law in regard to the phenomena of this world and its inevitable connection with unseen worlds and unseen conditions around us. For then, and then only, can suffering humanity be taught to distinguish between the real and the unreal, to separate the true from the false.

Occultism teaches, and the seer proves, that every one, both old and young, has immediately around him an ethereal envelope varying in colour, shape, and general appearance in accordance with his constitution, life, thoughts, and general aspirations. Within this atmosphere may be read the events of his past life, as also those which will happen in the future. It has been said before that every human being leaves behind him, as he goes through life, a train of circumstances, the actions of which were due to impulses originated in a previous incarnation. These circumstances can be seen in his atmosphere, the aura, itself being only visible in the astral light. Every movement we make, whether of importance or the reverse, must be in answer to a thought. If the movement is one of deep interest, on which much happiness or misery may depend, the mind dwells for a long time upon the subject, and fills in all the details necessary to the success of the project. Consequently, these thoughts get photographed in the astral light and whether they are thoughts, the results of which have been enacted, or whether the events consequent upon them are still to come, the seer can equally well read them, and thus foretell, very often, what will take place after a longer or shorter lapse of time. And, no matter how distant and apparently unconnected with the person whose aura is being examined may be he who is weaving in his mind the causes which will have such a great effect on his path through life, the clairvoyant can follow the subtle magnetic threads which link the two together with unerring skill.

What these magnetic currents, so real for the few who can perceive them, so unreal for mankind at large, are, the reader must discover for himself in the more advanced literature of this philosophy.

It is undoubtedly along these invisible threads that the master of the art of mental telegraphy reads his message; it is also by means of these lines that the mesmerist (unconsciously in this case) influences his sensitive when divided from him by many miles. A lock of hair given to a clairvoyant who is an absolute stranger to the owner of the hair, and separated by hundreds of miles, will enable him to send his mind along the magnetic currents which subsist between the hair and its natural possessor, so as to take note of what he is doing and what are his surroundings.

Thus it will be seen that Theosophy is not merely an abstract philosophy, dealing with metaphysics and fanciful theories, but that in it the student may surely find in this life the key to the hidden mysteries of nature, as well as the way that leads to spiritual and intellectual progress in the next state of existence.

## The Mahatmas

It has been already said that there are two classes of exceptionally constituted people who have within themselves certain phenomenal faculties, these being roughly defined as the trained and the untrained. The latter group, embracing seers, clairvoyants, and mediums, has been briefly dealt with, and it is now proposed to give the reader some information respecting the former group, that is to say, those who in addition to being born with some or all of the abnormal attributes above enumerated, have from youth upwards gone through a special course of training for the development of their psychical powers. It is commonly assumed that education on the physical plane renders an individual, whether exceptionally talented or the reverse, more capable of systematising his ideas, and more able to use them to advantage for the good of the human race, than if he is left to run wild, gathering his experiences in an unmethodical manner, and from perhaps untrustworthy sources, without proper instruction and assistance by those who have, by time and study, acquired practical and theoretical information in the well-beaten grooves of scholastic life. This being granted in regard to ordinary education, it is only rational to allow that experienced guidance and instruction is equally if not more necessary in the education of the spiritual faculties. That large numbers are at this moment going through such training and development, and others hoping to do so in the future, is at last recognised by some people in the West, and has in the East been an accepted fact from time immemorial.

The result of this psychological training is shown to its full extent in the Brotherhood to which the Mahatmas belong. The true seer or adept is enabled, in consequence of the special training he has gone through, to disembarrass his higher principles when engaged in the exercise of their faculties from all connection with the lower. The knowledge thus obtained can only be acquired or perceived in its integrity by these higher principles when they are unpolluted by attachment to the lower, and when approached by the untrained clairvoyant, is misconstrued and mixed up with the fancies and recollections of the physical brain, the functions of which, as an uninstructed psychic he does not know how to render, for the time being, inoperative. The passed adept, when in the state necessary for the reception of this sort of experience, is able to suspend the mechanical action of the brain, his spiritual sight thus becoming clear and uninfluenced by the admixture of the physical memory. This abstracted state is called in Hindu writings Samadhi, and is considered the highest condition of spirituality attainable by humanity while in the body. While on this subject it will be as well to quote again from *Isis Unveiled*: 'There are two kinds of seership, that of the soul and that of the spirit... But, as the visions of both depend upon the greater or less acuteness of the astral body, they differ very widely from the perfect omniscient spiritual state for, at best, the subject can get but glimpses of truth through the veil which physical nature interposes. The astral principle, or mind, called by the Hindu Yogin 'jivatma', is the sentient soul, inseparable from our physical brain, which it holds in subjection, and by which it is in its turn equally trammelled. This is the ego, the intellectual life-principle of man, his conscious entity... When the body is in the state of dharana - a total catalepsy of the physical frame - the soul of the clairvoyant may liberate itself and perceive things subjectively. And yet, as the sentient principle of the brain is alive and active, these pictures of the past, present, future will be tinctured with the terrestrial perceptions of the objective world; the physical memory and fancy will be in the way of clear vision. But the seer-adept knows how to suspend the mechanical action of the brain. His visions will be as clear as truth itself, uncoloured and undistorted, whereas the clairvoyant, unable to control the vibrations of the astral waves, will perceive but more or less broken images through the medium of the brain. The seer can never take flickering shadows for realities... He receives impressions directly from his spirit. Between his subjective and objective selves there are no obstructive mediums. This is the real spiritual seership, in which, according to an expression of Plato, soul is raised above all inferior good.'[11]

This psychological education which aspirants for admission into the community of adepts have to undergo is not given in a speculative or tentative manner, but is rather a regular mode of instruction, the rules for which are rigid and absolutely unavoidable, these having been in practice and handed down from one generation to another for thousands of years, since, indeed, humanity first evolved on this globe. The custodians of this school of knowledge are variously called Mahatmas, Rishis, Arhats, Adepts, Guru Devas, Brothers, etc, by their respective followers in different countries or religions, and contain within their number representatives of many nationalities. The majority of them now live in Tibet, although isolated members of the community are to be found elsewhere in far distant countries. They possess a knowledge of the hidden workings of Nature, and of the causes which produce the phenomena of the physical world. This enables them to produce, without other mechanism than their own will-power, phenomena that upset all the theories that workers in physical science have in the course of many years gradually built up, and are still acting upon. They can defy matter, distance, even death itself. They can create and disintegrate, that is to say, they are able to gather the elements out of the akasha[12] necessary for the production of material objects and cause them to become visible and tangible, as they can dissipate such objects into their original molecules, which at once diffuse themselves through the astral light and become invisible to the physical eye. They can take cognizance of people and their thoughts regardless of distance - impress, influence, and directly communicate with them. What the late Lord Lytton[13] in his *Coming Race*, described as vril power, the Mahatmas undoubtedly possess and can wield. They recognise and practically use for various psychological purposes the different principles spoken of previously as forming the constitution of man, and have in the routine of their training developed their higher principles while at the same time subduing the lower ones to such a state of perfection that the real spiritual man is independent of, and altogether master of, the material body, and can consequently leave it for long periods of time; the ego belonging thereto in the meantime acquiring real knowledge in other spheres, which on his return to earth goes to strengthen and support the block of such knowledge belonging to the brotherhood.

It is well known in India that fakirs and yogis can by the practice of asceticism and certain physical exercises, such as sitting for a long time together in a particular position, breathing at intervals laid down in accepted rules, etc, attain undoubtedly psychological powers and perform physical phenomena. This kind of training is called Hatha Yoga, while the higher description as taught by true adepts is called Raja Yoga. Between these two modes of education for the attainment of abnormal powers there is an enormous difference, the gap that separates the two, from the lowest form of the one to the highest of the other being filled in by followers of all the many and various religions and sects scattered over the whole of Asia. These include the juggler, who can perhaps practise a humble kind of sorcery for a small remuneration, and the holy man or yogi who lives an ascetic and solitary life, passing his time in meditation and religious practices, harming no one, but, on the contrary, doing good to the extent of bringing home to the uneducated people who visit him the desirability of leading a pure life now, in order that they may attain happiness in the future. But far above the best of these yogis - and that many of them are examples of passive holiness, spirituality, and purity there is no doubt - stand the Mahatmas. For they are the direct inheritors and guardians of the ancient wisdom-religion, and of the accumulated spiritual experience of those who have had charge of the world since humanity appeared thereon. And, when an aspirant to initiation reaches up to, and attains, adeptship, his further advancement and spiritual education is by no means at an end; for in spiritual culture, even more than in mundane, it would seem that the further a student goes, the wider grows the prospect before him. So that members of this venerated community, of which Europeans know so little, not only in their progress gain the personal and recorded wisdom of their contemporaries and predecessors, but they, as it were, test its accuracy as they go on step by step. And this intimacy with the working of the unseen hand that guides the universe - which gives to the adepts their supremacy in all matters relating to physical and other sciences - is acquired by them not as the aim and end of their aspirations, but accrues to them by degrees, while still chelas or neophytes in the line of study organised for their development, and is only a stepping-stone to the more sublime philosophy, acquaintanceship with which helps them to a comprehension of this divine and immutable law that reigns everywhere, alike both in the visible and invisible worlds around us, equally in things spiritual and physical. For just as it is impossible to find out the exact moment when mineral gives place to a vegetable growth or the vegetable becomes an animal, so it is likewise hopelessly difficult to determine the boundary which separates matter from spirit.

The attention of mankind may be, first of all, attracted to this brotherhood - the members of which have raised themselves to such a tremendous height above their fellow creatures - by the striking and overwhelming powers with which they are endowed but the student of their doctrine soon comes to regard even these as of inferior interest to the broad and enlightened views of the past and future of humanity, and its relation to and position in the scheme of the universe, to be obtained by their help. Their existence as human beings has been often, and still is, questioned by many; but on the other hand, hundreds of people have not only seen and spoken with them, but some have even lived under the same roof with their own Mahatmas for years together and naturally, during that time, have witnessed numberless instances of their powers in various directions. It is not, however, the purpose of this little book, as said before, to bring forward proofs of the statements made in it. These the reader can look for, and certainly find, elsewhere. But it may be mentioned, perhaps, in regard to this particular statement as to the existence of the adepts, that the student will find it not only supported in the Sacred Books of the East, which are replete with references to the 'Rishis' but also by the verbal assurance of reliable witnesses who have seen and conversed with their own adept-guru, both in the body and also astrally when separated by thousands of miles.

This separability of the astral from the material body in life is by no means so very uncommon even among Western people, who are quite unconnected with Eastern modes of training, and who have no knowledge of the Mahatmas. And it is perfectly well known among certain circles of society that this particular faculty is frequently resorted to by those still in life who wish to visit and communicate with their relatives and friends who have passed away into another state of existence. Moreover, two or more 'astrals' will make this journey in company, remembering accurately on their return to their respective bodies the conversations they have had with their dead friends, as well as the appearance and leading features of the scenery and country they have traversed in finding these friends. Therefore, if some among us can have such experiences without having gone through a life-long training, or having had any special guidance, why should the existence of the Brothers be doubted because their pupils maintain they get such astral visits from their 'masters' when they know that their bodies are hundreds of miles away. Again, if an untrained person finds that he can leave his body at will and traverse the invisible worlds around, bringing back the record of his travels and impressions, how much more possible it is to believe that the adept, who in addition to the natural qualities with which, like the seer, he is at birth in possession of, has been for long years devoting himself to their development, aided by the experience and knowledge of those who, for many generations past, have trodden the same path before him. And why should we find it unreasonable to suppose that these initiates should have within their keeping a transcendental philosophy which has for its foundation, truth and spiritual knowledge. It must be remembered, also, that adeptship is not the result of the work of one life, for the way up to that high point in human evolution cannot be attained in so short a time, even under the most favourable conditions; these conditions belonging to some of the many mysteries that have to be unriddled by a student in his way along the path that leads to a comprehension of occult science.

The first spark of interest in mysticism which gradually unfolds itself in any given individual by reading and study is probably due to some slight contact in a previous birth with people of like tendencies. The reading and theoretical education which he encourages in himself in this life will have its results in his next incarnation, when perhaps he will be strong enough to force himself, by his earnestness, purity of life, and spirituality, on the notice of a master, and eventually become a probationary chela. Once an accepted chela, his progress towards initiation depends upon the mental, physical, moral and intellectual attributes, which he may then develop; and there are many initiations to be passed through before adeptship is reached, which we are told is only achieved after a long and weary probation, during which period the man is tried, tested, and proved at every step in his upward course, not only in regard to all bodily desires and feelings, but also in regard to his mental and intellectual qualifications; for to be a Mahatma means to be the embodiment of knowledge, power and justice. It is the goal for which unconsciously humanity is struggling; to which the majority will eventually attain through the long course of trials, experiences and pleasures that all have to undergo in the birth and rebirth of the ego in its many incarnations.

Those who are anxious to shorten the journey to this far-distant haven of rest from earthly existence, can only do so by leaving the high way - which, though comparatively smooth and of easy ascent, is very long - and taking to the mountain paths that lead directly to the top, for those who are at the same time fearless and faithful.

## Rules for Students

It may now be advisable to give, for the guidance both of would-be chelas and those who only desire to become theoretical students of this philosophy, some information respecting the kind of life real chelaship entails, and what resemblance it bears to the lives led by ordinary people. Chelaship is much less infrequent in India than in almost any other country, and the reason of this lies on the surface, and is accounted for by the fact that belief in, and reverence for, the Mahatmas may be described as almost hereditary in Hindus. It goes hand in hand with a strong addiction to the study of transcendental metaphysics. This tendency is not confined to the upper classes of society, but is observable likewise in nearly every Hindu who has sufficient education. Even those who, in consequence of having received a Western education, call themselves Materialists and argue usually along the lines of Tyndall or Huxley, have, below their English methods of thought, a firm belief in the 'supernatural,' so-called, combined with an admiring devotion to the sacred literature of their own country. It naturally follows that candidates for occult training present themselves in considerable numbers. Entrance, however, into the channel that will lead to their acceptance as pupils is not so easy as might at first be imagined for the laws and regulations that guard the portals into this path are very stringent, and neither family ties nor worldly duties may be put aside or disregarded. Thus in India, early marriages are productive of great trouble in many cases. A young man whose earnest desire and hope is to become a chela may often find himself hopelessly cut off from following the only career for which he has any inclination by the fact that he has, dependent upon him, a wife whom he has hardly seen, and duties in life for which he is both unfitted and indisposed.

Let us, however, take a case in which there is no question of a wife. The aspirant for spiritual knowledge can, with the help of a master, begin the work before him, the master at first being only required to give him certain advice relative to exercises for the development of his psychical faculties, and to see that in their progress and growth he does not come to grief. For such exercises, taken by one eager to acquire personal development, and persevered in without proper guidance, lay him open to the various influences resident in the unseen world, which, unless he is protected by a strong, trained will-force, are liable to gather round him and produce very dangerous results.

Simultaneously with these mental exercises, the neophyte must confine himself to a simple diet of grain, milk and vegetables, taken only in moderate quantities and at stated intervals. This restraint over his desire to eat and drink one sort of food in preference to another is quite the smallest and humblest commencement of the difficulties that beset the upward life. For he must not only have complete control over the emotions consequent on the material pleasures and pains of ordinary life but he must also learn to conquer or rise above mental suffering, he must not only strive to become indifferent to mental and physical weaknesses but he must succeed in doing so, otherwise there is no hope of his advancement in that particular incarnation. He who sets out with the intention of making occultism the study of his life, and adeptship the goal of that study, whether in this or a future incarnation, has to acquire, at all events to some extent, the four accomplishments called in Brahminical books the four *Sadhanas*.[14] These accomplishments carry in their attainment complete mastery over all the material desires, either of the body or the mind, which pertain to the personality; they also bring in their train spiritual enlightenment which enables the chela to comprehend in some measure the oneness of the universe and his own connection therewith. The first accomplishment gives to the neophyte the power to distinguish between the real and the unreal, and to grasp intellectually the fact that every thing connected with corporeal life on this planet is but transitory, and therefore *not the real*. The second is in a measure the result or consequence of the first, for, the firm conviction of the transient character of this existence once truly established in the pupil's mind, all desire for the pleasures arising from it leave him, and he thus acquires the second accomplishment, which is, entire indifference to the results of actions, or to the praise and blame accruing therefrom. He escapes even from the desire for life excepting as a means to the acquisition of spiritual knowledge.

The third accomplishment embraces the six qualifications, which are briefly as follows:

1. Mental abstinence, i.e. the subjugation of all evil feelings such as envy, hatred, malice, revenge, and the purification of the mind of all worldly anxieties.

2. Bodily abstinence, this, it will be seen, must be the necessary consequence of the first, for as all actions are prompted by thoughts, these latter having been trained to dwell entirely upon spiritual subjects, and with the wish to benefit humanity, it naturally follows that the daily life of the chela will be not only free from all kinds of vice or selfishness, but that his body will, without effort, conform to the ascetic rules laid down as essential to the development of man's psychical and spiritual faculties.

3. Freedom from all bigotry, or preference for one form of religion over another, the aspirant being then able to sympathise with and assist all classes equally.

4. Perennial cheerfulness arising from the absence of all pride, having no wish for praise, being without resentment when blamed or wrongly

accused, nor caring to prove himself right or another person wrong, and the readiness to part with everything he possesses.

5. The attainment of this qualification renders the chela incapable of deviating from the right path, for he has by this time obtained such complete control over the senses and cravings of his body and mind, that the motives that tempt the generality of humanity, in their way through life, to pursue pleasure, ambition, and wealth, at any cost, no longer have any hold over him, and he can consequently pass through every sort of temptation without danger of being attracted out of the road that leads to adeptship.

6. A full and perfect belief in his own power of receiving spiritual knowledge, and of the ability of his adept-guru to teach him this science.

The fourth and last accomplishment necessary to attain is an ardent longing for spiritual freedom and liberation from conditioned existence.[15]

It will be readily acknowledged that, these accomplishments achieved, the chela will be in an advanced state of spirituality as compared with humanity at large, and that, even if he got no further, his condition, morally, would be one of immense superiority as contrasted with the best among us who are held up as patterns of holiness. But, while in his endeavours to purify his lower nature, he has at the same time been acquiring a knowledge of his higher attributes, and has in a measure been enabled to look over, if not to cross, that gulf which Mr. Herbert Spencer affirms must for ever separate us, as finite beings, from knowledge of the unknowable but only Reality. The chela has by this time triumphed over the difficulties that surround and beset the way from probationary to accepted chelaship. For a person no sooner gets recognised as a probationary chela, and begins his preparatory studies, than, as a natural consequence of the situation, all the evil qualities and attributes pertaining to his personality spring into view. Propensities of which his friends and probably he himself were not previously aware, now assert themselves, and either develop or are crushed, according to the moral power and strength of will of the person in question. If, after several chances have been given him, he is found unable to resist temptation or to conquer his desires, he is finally rejected by his master as incompetent to take a place in the ranks of accepted chelas. The latter, however, having safely passed this critical period, go on in the way laid down for them, each in turn tested and tried in every way that their individual weakness may suggest. Sometimes they are found wanting, fail at some of the minor initiations which they have to pass, and get thrown back for a time. In other cases they advance quickly, as their Karma dictates, or, in other words, as their strength of will and ardent desire urge them on to the higher ranks, due to the affinities which their former lives attracted round them. At all events, the road up to adeptship is so arduous and difficult that only a very small percentage of those who offer themselves, and are accepted for training, can reach the top in one or even two or three incarnations.

Of those who struggle along as chelas all their lives, without attaining complete or more than partial success, many, if not all, see their way to it later on, and in the meantime are so freed from the trammels and necessities of physical existence, that time for them assumes a new aspect, and they can very well afford to wait for the future, conscious of the support and assistance of their revered masters that await them at the all-important moment.

If the reader has followed the Theosophic teaching accurately, as thus far sketched out, he will have discovered that the fate of mankind is a long succession of re-births, interspersed with longer or shorter spells of spiritual and blissful existence, or semi-unconsciousness, in exact proportion as their lives on earth were given to material or higher tendencies. One of the aims of the neophyte, in his struggle for adeptship, is then to shorten the number of his incarnations, and, by so doing, to get into a state of existence to which, in the ordinary course of evolution, man will not attain but through the lapse of millions of years; for we are told that the minimum length of time between one incarnation and another for average adult humanity is about one thousand five hundred years.

The chela, by a system of forced or artificial incarnations, foregoes his very large share of heaven, which share has been enormously increased by his exceptionally spiritual life, and thus rapidly gains that status in the universe to which, in the customary flow of human spiritual progress, he would only attain, as said previously, in millions of years.

The artificial incarnation alluded to will be less difficult to comprehend by those who know or have any experience of the separability of the astral from the physical body before described. Not only can a Mahatma in this way leave his body, but he can also enter the body of one of his chelas, making use of these strange organs almost as if they were his own, the chela's astral in the meantime being absent. Thus the physical body of a chela, which is eventually worn out before the entity is sufficiently advanced for initiation, may with the aid of his adept master be transplanted into another body more fitted to carry on the work begun in the previous one. The body chosen for this purpose would be one that in the process of nature has lost its vital principle from some one of the many cases due to illness and disease. At the moment of what is commonly spoken of as dissolution, the strange ego takes possession of its new case, and has to conform to its shape, proclivities, etc, moulding these latter by degrees to the necessities of the new situation. The Teshu Lama of Thibet,[16] the head of the occult hierarchy, is always a reincarnation of this sort, the body of a quite young baby being taken for this particular ceremony. The Teshu Lama is, of course, an adept of high standing, and when, as happens in the course of years, his body becomes too frail for further occupation, he reincarnates in the body of a baby. The following account of Captain Turner's[17] interview with an infant Teshu Lama in 1783, is taken from Mr. Clements Markham's book on Thibet,[18] and may interest the reader as illustrative of this occult practice of immediate reincarnation:

'On the morning of the 4th of December the British envoy had his audience, and found the princely child, then aged eighteen months, seated on a throne with his father and mother standing on the left hand. Having been informed that although unable to speak he could understand, Captain Turner said, 'that the Governor-General, on receiving the news of his decease in China, was overwhelmed with grief and sorrow, and continued to lament his absence from the world until the cloud that had overcast the happiness of this nation was dispelled by his reappearance, and then, if possible, a greater degree of joy had taken place than he had experienced grief on receiving the first mournful news...' The infant looked steadfastly at the British envoy, with the appearance of much attention, and nodded with repeated but slow motions of the head, as though he understood every word. He was silent and sedate, his whole attention was directed to the envoy, and he conducted himself with astonishing dignity and decorum. He was one of the handsomest children Captain Turner had ever seen, and he grew up to be an able and devout ruler, delighting the Thibetans with his presence for many years, and dying at a good old age.'[19]

The individuality of the Dalai Lama, who must be also an adept, is probably carried on in the same way as that of the Teshu Lama. It is hardly probable that these forced incarnations take place in the West, although occasionally cases may be heard of that seem to suggest the possibility. In the East, however, they are by no means of such very uncommon occurrence, as may be ascertained in various ways by the persevering inquirer. Consequently, when it was said above that adeptship was seldom if ever accomplished in one life, it was not meant by that statement that the chela was allowed to die in the usual way and bide his time for re-birth in the accustomed manner, taking up his training where he had dropped it some two or three thousand years before, but that he hoped for the chance of carrying on his spiritual progress without any break of continuity.

One of the objects, therefore, that chelas have in view will have now been sufficiently elucidated, and the fight at first to be made against the claims and selfishness of the body, though difficult, once accomplished, the result is proportionately great.

The next questions to be considered are, what the general run of mankind gain by merely a theoretical study of this philosophy, what inducements can lead them to take up new lines of thought, and how, while still living an ordinary life, people may still follow out some of the rules laid down for the guidance of chelas, and with what result on their future. One of the first truths the upward-striving soul has to realise is the temporary character of the body or personality, as compared with the individuality, which is the real and lasting part of the human being. He must also recognise the continuance of the consciousness of the individuality in each successive birth, in spite of the personal memory being absent, and the philosophical necessity for those primary rules of general morality, comprising unselfishness, charity, justice, etc, as taught by all religions. A third conception to be grasped is the necessity of a firm belief in the Divine element within us, which may be either encouraged or repressed, according to the means taken for promoting either result. These lessons the ordinary student may try to follow and profit by equally with the chela, certainly with profit to himself in his next birth, and to the immediate advantage of those around him. But a life of unsystematic innocence, no matter how free from actual sin, nor how devotional in spirit, would have comparatively little effect on the evolutionary progress of the entity. Without a certain amount of study towards the comprehension of spiritual science, there would be no advance for the entity beyond that which all well-intentioned people make unconsciously and by slow degrees forward. These will ensure a certain phase of conscious spiritual life (i.e. spiritual as being free from the material body), dependent upon their various higher attributes, and a reincarnation afterwards exactly suited for the working out of their Karma, more or less laden with happiness or the reverse as dictated by their previous actions. The intellectual study of the esoteric doctrine, therefore, taken quite separately from anything like personal training of the psychical faculties, is an important factor in evolutionary progress. Conducing, as it does, moreover, to a moral and unselfish life, intellectual work in the study of esoteric science must stimulate the future spiritual progress of the entity to an enormous extent. Without supposing any extra number of incarnations for the intellectual worker on spiritual lines, the mere fact that his life has been passed in the acquisition of such knowledge should carry with it an exceedingly protracted existence in Devachan (the Thibetan equivalent for Heaven), where, during this time, he will not be simply in a state of blissful but unprogressive happiness, but where he will be continuing, only under much more favourable conditions, the work which was the main interest of his earthly life. This protracted existence in Devachan naturally lands the ego, when his time comes for re-birth, in a period of advanced spirituality, as compared with that of the Earth when he last left it, the progress being due to many thousands of years that have passed since his last incarnation, during which time humanity has been developing the resources of science, as also their own psychical faculties. The returning ego does not find itself unprepared for the great difference in the condition of humanity, consequent on its extra long existence in Devachan; but it is quite abreast of, if not still in advance of, the stream, without having gone through the many incarnations which have been necessary to the majority of mankind to bring them to this stage of their journey. In this way the study of spiritual philosophy must reduce the ego's number of incarnations, though not on the same lines, nor with the same complete success, as the more elaborate training of the chela. The main consideration, therefore, for the reader to bear in mind is, that without some distinct and sustained effort in one direction or another, whether over the physical body or in mental work, no exceptional progress can be made by any person in the human procession that is marching on towards that point in the development which the Mahatmas have already reached. Obedience to a moral code, the regular performance of all daily duties, an attitude of uncritical devotion to religious forms and customs, are all very praiseworthy actions, inasmuch as they spring from the dictates of the person's conscience, and are no doubt as examples productive of good; but in themselves they will not urge forward the entity out of the beaten track, nor guide it into the channels leading to quicker methods of advancement in the next incarnation. While in such a groove the ego will not retrograde, and thus run the risk of dropping out of the procession altogether, but it will keep in the ranks instead of pushing forward.

Those who cannot by reason of family ties or other occupations enter on the direct path of chelaship, although with the strong impulse in their natures to do so, may make sure progress by the theoretical study of occultism in all its branches, and this they may without breaking natural bonds or without disturbing the comfort of either friends or relations; they may also do this unostentatiously, and yet eventually with the best results. And if their ardent hope is to achieve a regular chelaship sooner or later, let them keep that idea well in mind, acting up, as far as their position in regard to others dependent upon them will allow, to the rules laid down for the guidance of chelas. Such persons can always get advice and assistance from those in advance of them in these matters; and, if they should be members of the Theosophical Society, will obtain such help with all the greater facility.

It will, perhaps, be as well to mention here, that in the formation of the Theosophical Society the founders were acting under the direct wishes of certain of the Mahatmas, who thus opened the occult door a little way for those whose intuitions were sufficiently active to guide them to take advantage of this source of knowledge. The society, which in India has spread with extraordinary rapidity, has been of immense service to the people of that country by arousing in them love and respect for their own ancient literature and philosophy (which through the diffusion of western modes of thought and education, had become almost dormant), thus raising their self-respect and patriotism. Should the Society spread also among the Anglo-Indian community residing in that country, it would prove a bond of union and sympathy between the two peoples.

In the West, the Society has had success of a different kind than in the East, and it has given, what is now seen to have been so urgently required, an indication showing in what direction the knowledge and explanation of mystic literature was to be found. It has been already noticed that in the West the proof of the existence of the Mahatmas is not considered satisfactory, and even some members within the Society may still remain unconvinced of the fact. Nevertheless, the Mahatmas are its real founders, and in close connection with its nominal leaders. To show the divergent way in which people may look at the same question, it is amusing to find that in India the Hindus had first to be convinced, not of the actual existence of the Mahatmas as living men, for of this they had ample proof, but that the visible founders of the Society were really their agents and in communication with them. This once proved to the satisfaction of the Hindus, all went well, and there are branches in active working order in almost every town in the three Presidencies of

India, while in Ceylon the movement has taken, if possible still firmer root. Owing to the energetic measures started by Colonel Olcott in this island, he has, in addition to winning over great numbers of adherents to the Society, been the means of organising and bringing into active working order many Buddhist schools where local children can now obtain a good education. Formerly these children had either to be sent to schools presided over by Christian missionaries, or they had to go without any regular instruction. Those parents who felt they could trust to the home influence counteracting what they considered the dangers to the religious beliefs of their boys and girls arising from such education, sent them, wisely taking the good and rejecting what, from their point of view, was the bad. Others, incapable of seeing anything but the dangers of possible perversion, kept their children at home, the result being that thousands of the Singhalese boys and girls were growing up in a state of hopeless ignorance. This evil has now, in a great measure, been removed, and in Ceylon, as in western countries, the children can now go to schools presided over by masters holding the same religious beliefs as their parents.

In Europe, the Theosophical movement is not a simple revival of this kind. The views of Nature to which it leads, present themselves at first, it is true, amongst us, as new ideas. But even amongst us, when the matter is rightly considered, Theosophy may be regarded as a revival - a revival, that is to say, of the real esoteric meaning embodied in the principal religion of the West as well as in those of the East. Western dogmas have disguised the Esoteric Doctrine very elaborately, but it still runs through them for those who are able to appreciate it. Its outlines may be traced as clearly in Christianity as in the faith of Thibet. For many Theosophists this matters very little. Their interest lies in the study of abstract truth, and not in the dissensions that have given rise to antagonistic theological systems. Still, it would be a mistake to imagine that abstract speculation supplies the only method by which the truth can be approached. It can be sought in the analysis of old, as well as in the construction of new creeds, and having regard to the probability that large numbers of educated men and women, whether Christians, Buddhists, or

Brahmins, might find it difficult to give intelligible reasons for preferring their own to rival formulas, the consideration that Theosophy seeks its purpose - the cultivation of spirituality - in detecting identities rather than in emphasising contrasts, may perhaps put the movement on friendly terms with many people who might otherwise wrongly imagine themselves bound to offer it their opposition.

1. Appanage, a benefit or right belonging to someone.

2. Helena Petrovna Blavatsky, *Isis Unveiled, vol II*, J. W. Bouton, New York, 1877.

3. Helena Petrovna Blavatsky, *Isis Unveiled, vol I*, J. W. Bouton, New York, 1877. Merkabah/Merkavah mysticism (or Chariot mysticism) is a school of early Jewish mysticism, c. 100 BC - 1000 AD, inspired by visions such as those found in the 'Book of Ezekiel Chapter 1', or in the heikhalot ('palaces') literature, concerning stories of ascents to the heavenly palaces and the Throne of God. The main corpus of the Merkavah literature was composed in the period 200 - 700 AD, although later references to the Chariot tradition can also be found in the literature of the Chassidei Ashkenaz in the Middle Ages. A major text in this tradition is the *Maaseh Merkabah (Work of the Chariot)*.

4. *The Nineteenth Century* was a British monthly literary magazine founded in 1877 by Sir James Knowles. Many of the early contributors to *The Nineteenth Century* were members of the Metaphysical Society. The journal was established to publish debate by leading intellectuals.

5. Friedrich Max Müller (6 December 1823 - 28 October 1900) was a German-born philologist who lived and studied in Britain for most of his life. He was one of the founders of the western academic field of Indian studies. Müller wrote both scholarly and popular works on the subject of Indology. *The Sacred Books of the East*, a fifty-volume set of English translations, was prepared under his direction.

6. Professor John William Draper (5 May 1811 - 4 January 1882) was an English-American scientist, philosopher, physician, chemist, historian and photographer. He is credited with producing the first clear photograph of a female face, 1839 - 40, and the first detailed photograph of the moon in 1840. He is the author of *History of the Conflict Between Religion and Science* published in 1874.

7. Zeno of Citium (c. 334 BC - c. 262 BC) was a Hellenistic thinker from Citium (Kition), Cyprus, and probably of Phoenician descent. Zeno was the founder of the Stoic school of philosophy, which he presided over in Athens from about 300 BC. Based on the moral ideas of the Cynics, Stoicism placed great emphasis on goodness and peace of mind gained from living a life of virtue in accordance with nature. It proved very successful and flourished as the dominant philosophy from the Hellenistic period to the Roman era.

8. Herbert Spencer (27 April 1820 - 8 December 1903) was an English philosopher, biologist, anthropologist, sociologist, and prominent classical liberal political theorist of the Victorian era.

9. An elementary is a shell, an echo of a departed person which displays reverberations of his or her personality traits. These echoes are spontaneous with only the appearance of intelligence. An elementary is a residual presence.

10. Helena Petrovna Blavatsky, *Isis Unveiled, vol I*, J. W. Bouton, New York, 1877.

11. Helena Petrovna Blavatsky, *Isis Unveiled, vol II*, J. W. Bouton, New York, 1877.

12. According to theosophy, akasha is the spiritual primordial substance that pervades the whole of space, and from which the cosmos is developed.

13. Edward George Earle Lytton Bulwer-Lytton, 1st Baron Lytton, PC (25 May 1803 - 18 January 1873) was an English writer and politician. His novel *The Coming Race* was published anonymously in 1871. It also appeared under the title, *Vril, the Power of the Coming Race*. Some readers have accepted the account of a superior subterranean race and the energy-form called 'Vril' as a literal truth, at least in part. Some theosophists, notably Helena Blavatsky, William Scott-Elliot, and Rudolf Steiner, accepted the book as partly based on occult truth.

14. Sadhana, literally 'a means of accomplishing something', is a generic term from the yogic tradition. It refers to any spiritual exercise that is aimed at progressing the aspirant towards the ultimate expression of his or her life in this reality. It includes a variety of disciplines in Hindu, Buddhist, Jain and Sikh traditions that are followed in order to achieve various spiritual or ritual objectives.

15. For more information about these four accomplishments, see A.P. Sinnett, *Transactions of the London Lodge of the Theosophical Society, No. 1.*, 1895.

16. The Teshu Lama or The Panchen Lama is the reincarnate custodian of the Gelug school of Tibetan Buddhism. 'Panchen' is a portmanteau word combining 'Pandita' and 'Chenpo' meaning 'Great Scholar'. The Panchen Lama is one of the most important figures in the Gelug tradition, second only in authority to the Dalai Lama.

17. Samuel Turner FRS (19 April 1759 - 2 January 1802) was an English Asiatic traveller and the author of *An Account of an Embassy to the Court of the Teshoo Lama in Tibet, containing a Narrative of a Journey through Bootan and part of Tibet*, published in London, 1800.

18. Sir Clements Robert Markham KCB FRS (20 July 1830 - 30 January 1916) was an English geographer, explorer, and writer. He was secretary of the Royal Geographical Society between 1863 and 1888, and later served as the Society's president.

19. Clements Markham, *Narratives of the Mission of George Bogle to Tibet and the Journey of Thomas Manning to Lhasa*, Trubner & Co, London, 1876.

www.ingramcontent.com/pod-product-compliance
Ingram Content Group UK Ltd.
Pitfield, Milton Keynes, MK11 3LW, UK
UKHW022132220326
11407UKWH00010B/64/J